THE DESERT IS MY MOTHER

EL DESIERTO ES MI MADRE

BY PAT MORA
ART BY DANIEL LECHON

Piñata Books
A Division of Arte Público Press
University of Houston
Houston, Texas 77204

For my mother's other children, Cissy, Stella, and Anthony.

Pat Mora

Publication of *The Desert Is My Mother* is made possible through support from the Andrew W. Mellon Foundation, the Lila Wallace-Reader's Digest Fund and the National Endowment for the Arts. We are grateful for their support.

Esta edición de *El desierto es mi madre* ha sido subvencionada por la Fundación Andrew W. Mellon, el Fondo Lila Wallace-Reader's Digest y el Fondo Nacional para las Artes. Les agradecemos su apoyo.

Piñata Books are full of surprises!

Piñata Books
An Imprint of Arte Público Press
University of Houston
Houston, Texas 77204-2174

Design and Illustrations by Daniel Lechón

Mora, Pat.
    The desert is my mother = El desierto es mi madre / by Pat Mora ; illustrated by Daniel Lechón.
      p.   cm.
    Summary: A poetic depiction of the desert as the provider of comfort, food, spirit, and life.
    ISBN 1-55885-121-6: $14.95 Hardbound
    1. Deserts–Juvenile poetry. 2. Children's poetry, American–Translations into Spanish. 3. Children's poetry, American.
[1. Deserts–Poetry. 2. American poetry. 3. Spanish language materials–Bilingual.] I. Lechón, Daniel, ill. II. Title. III. Title: Desierto es mi madre.
PS3563.073D47   1994
811'.54–dc20   94-20047
                                                        CIP
                                                         AC

1 2 3 4 5 6 7 8 9 0   11 10 9 8 7 6 5

THE DESERT IS MY MOTHER

EL DESIERTO ES MI MADRE

I say feed me.

She serves red prickly pear on a spiked cactus.

Le digo, dame de comer.

Me sirve rojas tunas en nopal espinoso.

I say tease me.

She sprinkles raindrops in my face
on a sunny day.

Le digo, juguetea conmigo.

Me salpica la cara con gotitas de lluvia
en día asoleado.

I say frighten me.

She shouts thunder, flashes lightning.

Le digo, asústame.

Me grita con truenos y me tira relámpagos.

I say hold me.

She whispers, "Lie in my arms."

Le digo, abrázame.

Me susurra, "Acuéstate aquí".

I say heal me.

She gives me chamomile, oregano, peppermint.

Le digo, cúrame.

Me da manzanilla, orégano y yerbabuena.

I say caress me.

She strokes my skin with her warm breath.

Le digo, acaríciame.

Me roza la cara con su cálido aliento.

I say make me beautiful.

She offers turquoise for my fingers,
a pink blossom for my hair.

Le digo, hazme bella.

Me ofrece turquesa para mis dedos,
una flor rosada para mi cabello.

I say sing to me.

She chants her windy songs.

Le digo, cántame.

Me arrulla con sus canciones de viento.

I say teach me.

She blooms in the sun's glare,
the snow's silence,
the driest sand.

Le digo, enséñame.

Y florece en el brillo del sol,
en el silencio de la nieve,
en las arenas más secas.

Campbell Hall
The Ahmanson Library

The desert is my mother.

El desierto es mi madre.

The desert is my strong mother.

El desierto es mi madre poderosa.

The Desert Is My Mother

I say feed me.
She serves red prickly pear on a spiked cactus.

I say tease me.
She sprinkles raindrops in my face on a sunny day.

I say frighten me.
She shouts thunder, flashes lightning.

I say hold me.
She whispers, "Lie in my arms."

I say heal me.
She gives me chamomile, oregano, peppermint.

I say caress me.
She strokes my skin with her warm breath.

I say make me beautiful.
She offers turquoise for my fingers,
      a pink blossom for my hair.

I say sing to me.
She chants her windy songs.

I say teach me.
She blooms in the sun's glare,
      the snow's silence,
      the driest sand.

The desert is my mother.
El desierto es mi madre.

The desert is my strong mother.

El desierto es mi madre

Le digo, dame de comer.
Me sirve rojas tunas en nopal espinoso.

Le digo, juguetea conmigo.
Me salpica la cara con gotitas de lluvia en día asoleado.

Le digo, asústame.
Me grita con truenos y me tira relámpagos.

Le digo, abrázame.
Me susurra, "Acuéstate aquí".

Le digo, cúrame.
Me da manzanilla, orégano y yerbabuena.

Le digo, acaríciame.
Me roza la cara con su cálido aliento.

Le digo, hazme bella.
Me ofrece turquesa para mis dedos,
        una flor rosada para mi cabello.

Le digo, cántame.
Me arrulla con sus canciones de viento.

Le digo, enséñame.
Y florece en el brillo del sol,
        en el silencio de la nieve,
        en las arenas más secas.

El desierto es mi madre.
El desierto es mi madre.

El desierto es mi madre poderosa.

Pat Mora

Pat Mora is the most renowned Hispanic poet for children, young adults and adults. Two of her three poetry books, *Chants* and *Borders*, have won the Southwest Book Award as did her children's book, *A Birthday Basket for Tía*. Among her other titles for children are *Listen to the Desert: Oye el desierto* and *Pablo's Tree*. Mora is a fellow of the National Endowment for the Arts and the W.K. Kellogg Foundation. She is the mother of three children.

Pat Mora es la más celebrada de los poetas hispanos para niños, jóvenes y adultos. Su libro infantil *Una canasta de cumpleaños para Tía* y sus poemarios *Chants* (Cantos) y *Borders* (Fronteras), han recibido el premio Southwest Book Award. Mora es autora de otros libros infantiles: *Pablo's Tree* (El árbol de Pablo) y *Listen to the Desert: Oye el desierto*. Mora es becada del Fondo Nacional para las Artes y la Fundación W.K. Kellogg. La escritora tiene tres hijos.

Daniel Lechón

Daniel Lechón is a prize-winning artist whose works have been collected and exhibited in museums and galleries in the United States and Mexico. Lechón received his Masters Degree in Fine Arts from the University of Mexico in 1949. Lechón currently resides in Houston, Texas, where he shares his talents as an illustrator for Arte Público Press and continues to produce fine works for exhibit and sale.

Las obras de Daniel Lechón se han coleccionado y expuesto en museos y galerías en los Estados Unidos y México. Lechón, quien recibió título de Maestro de Artes Plásticas de la Universidad de México, reside en el presente en Houston, Texas. Dedicado a su labor artística, el maestro colabora con sus diseños e illustraciones para Arte Público Press.

Piñata Books

An Imprint of Arte Público Press

University of Houston

Houston, Texas 77204-2174

Piñata Books are full of surprises!